freebie.robloxiakid.com/r

DIARY OF A ROBLOX NOOB

BEE SWARM SIMULATOR

ROBLOXIA KID

Contents

1   It's Tough Being a Noob.   1

2   Trouble in the Fields and a Magic Tool.   9

3   From Bad to Worse.   15

4   And then…   24

5   The Attack of the Ants.   34

6   The Werewolf.   43

7   The Giant Mantis.   61

8   A Great Surprise.   69

Entry #1

It's Tough Being a Noob.

"Boy, this new game is something else!"

Yeah, that was me whining and complaining. I'm not usually one to complain or whine about any game I play in Roblox. After all, I've played just about every Roblox game there is to play, and then some! By the way, my name's Noob if you haven't caught it yet.

So, what was this really tough game I was complaining about? It was Bee Simulator, of course. Basically, it's about growing your hive and getting the best bees to make you a lot of honey. Basically, it's all about getting the best bee for your buck. Haha, okay, I know, I know, that joke was just way off.

Anyway, I *was* complaining, but don't get me wrong here. Bee Simulator is no bad game, not by a long shot. If anything, it's probably the opposite of a bad game. It's amazing. The payoff of building a large hive and having all those cool bees work with you is something else. It's something I would love to get. It's just so tough; I mean, I just don't know where to begin.

"Come on, let's get moving to make that honey!"

I was moving around the field and gathering more stuff for my bees to make honey. Yeah, I wasn't really doing a good job of it, but neither were my bees. I guess we were all just really off. There was no unity in our actions. We weren't doing this very well.

"Cut us a little slack here, boss! The boys are

trying their best but it's not easy to make all that honey!"

The big yellow bee I was speaking to? That was my only rare bee. It was a bumblebee and his name was Nate. Yeah, he was my only bee of real importance in the hive. He was the only rare bee in my hive that was full of plain, old common bees. Not only did I not have any rare bees aside from Nate, but I also didn't have any epic or legendary bees to my name. Let's not even talk about event bees which were probably the rarest, strongest and coolest bee type. If you had bees like this, you were basically a legendary bee master. Well, I guess it really was no surprise why my hive wasn't producing as much honey as I wanted.

"Come on, Nate! You guys can make a lot more honey if you just put your backs into it!"

Nate shook his head.

"You think it's easy making all that honey? You try being a bee like us!"

I guess Nate had a point there. I mean, I was really getting on their case, but if you thought about it, they were really doing the best that they could. A single rare bee and a lot of common bees could only do so much. I needed to get more powerful bees if I wanted my hive to go anywhere.

I was really just getting mad at Nate and the boys out of sheer frustration. I guess I was becoming something of a bad boss to my poor bees. Yeah, I know, it wasn't right and it wasn't one of my best moments. Still, I couldn't help myself. Despite my best efforts, the hive wasn't producing as much honey as I wanted, and I was really looking like, well, a Noob in all of this. It was beyond embarrassing.

To make matters worse, I was sharing the same pollen field with another, much more experienced player. Mario. Mario was the complete opposite of myself in Bee Simulator. Where I was, well, a Noob, Mario was a real pro. He had amassed the biggest and most productive hive in all of Bee Simulator. His hive was so big, you could see it several miles away from the field. The hive was also full of the best and most productive bees ever seen anywhere. I only had one rare bee to handle all of the common bees in my hive, but Mario had several. His rare bees were the ones who did the bulk of the work in the hive, but he also had several epic and legendary bees as well. What he didn't have was an event bee, but that didn't really seem to matter. After all, event bees were pretty rare already, and his hive was already killing it, even without one.

"'Ey! Good morning neighbor! Am I

interrupting some serious work there?"

Mario had a strange European accent, along with a thick moustache and a large belly. He also always dressed in red and blue. I could have sworn that I had seen him in another game, but maybe that was just me.

"We're fine Mario."

I was definitely more than a little annoyed. I didn't like Mario dropping in like this and butting into my business. If anything, Mario seemed to be more than a little dense. The guy always seemed to be butting in when I didn't really want him to be around. His annoying nature only made me even more jealous of his success at the server.

"You sure, neighbor? You seemed to be getting on poor Nate's case. I mean, take it from me. If you really want your bees to perform well, you can't go treating them badly. Not that it's any of my business."

"You're right, Mario. It's none of your business."

Yeah, I was really straight to the point and beyond blunt there, but I just couldn't help myself. Mario was really getting on my nerves, even if he didn't mean to.

"Whoa! Isn't that a bit harsh?"

Maybe it was, but I was just so frustrated. I mean, if it wasn't bad enough that my bees were all performing way below expected, I just had to be sharing the same field with one of the top players of the game! That was like rubbing salt on an open wound. Maybe Mario didn't mean to get on my nerves, but I just couldn't help but feel bad about all of this.

"You probably think you're some really cool master player of the game, Mario! Well, let me tell you now, you're not! You're not as cool as you think! You should go crawl down a pipe and face a turtle or something!"

Mario seemed to smile under his thick moustache.

"Been there, done that."

"Yeah, what do you mean by that?"

Before Mario could even answer, something came up that made my day even worse than it already was.

"Everybody run! It's a giant ladybug!"

Nate yelled the warning as my bees flew away in all directions. They all knew the ladybug was trouble, and so did I.

Entry #2

Trouble in the Fields and a Magic Tool.

"Run! Save yourselves! There's a giant ladybug coming!"

Being a bee wasn't sweets and honey all the time in Bee Simulator. There was always the chance that your poppy field would be invaded by several giant mobs that were pretty dangerous to bees, and even beekeepers like myself. Yep, the giant ladybug was just another example of that kind of mob.

I turned around and saw the giant ladybug coming our way. It was a giant one, all right. She was big, red and very nasty looking. She looked as if she could eat a bee just by looking at it.

"A giant ladybug! Come on, Mario!"

I motioned for Mario to move away, but he didn't budge an inch. He remained standing right where he was and stared the giant ladybug down. I couldn't see any kind of fear in Mario's eyes. I'm ashamed to admit that I was the complete opposite; there was just a whole lot of fear in my eyes and I wanted to get out of there as fast as I could.

"What are you standing around for, Mario? Come on! That giant ladybug isn't messing around. If we stay here, she could trample on us, or even eat us!"

Mario didn't say anything and just remained standing there. I was shaking in my boots already, but he wouldn't move. He wasn't afraid at all.

"I'm not going anywhere. You take another step and I'm going to trample on you real good!" he said.

The giant ladybug smiled at Mario. She wasn't afraid of his threat. In fact, she seemed amused that this small and plump man would dare to challenge her.

Without thinking twice, the ladybug took another step towards us.

"All right! That's it! You asked for it!" Mario said.

Mario ran right towards the giant ladybug. He didn't hesitate at all.

"Mario! What are you doing?"

Mario didn't answer. His eyes were completely focused on the ladybug as he moved straight towards her. As he ran towards the giant bug, the giant bug ran towards him. It was kind of like two lightning bolts colliding with each other, or two giant trains driving straight at each other. Or two… well, you get the picture.

"Mamma Mia! I'm coming right at you, you dumb bug!"

At the last moment, Mario jumped over the bug's head and landed right on top of it. He landed with so much force that the giant bug was squished. It was actually kind of awesome seeing Mario do that.

"Well, that takes care of that giant pest!" he said.

He squished the giant ladybug and a huge roar erupted from the bees. His bees and even my bees were cheering Mario. This was beyond embarrassing now. I just felt completely useless. What was the point of even trying to get better? How could I beat someone who could flatten ladybugs?

"What are you guys cheering about? Get back to work!" I barked.

Nate and the others were stunned silent. I had never been that harsh to my bees. This was a first even for me. Looking back, I admit that I'm really ashamed of my behavior, but back then I didn't feel any kind of shame at all. I was simply angry, frustrated, and jealous. I didn't have a clue how I could get better at Bee Simulator and get my hive to become more productive.

"Take it easy, Noob! Bees don't like to be treated that way. Nobody does!"

"What do you care? You're the dude with the best hive! I can't possibly measure up to you."

Mario shook his head.

"You don't have to be angry like this, Noob. You can get better. I can show you how to get as good as me. There's a magic tool that can increase bee production. Your bees will be making honey like hotcakes with it and..."

I raised my hand and shook my head.

"I think you've already done enough, Mario," I said.

Yep, that was the end of that conversation. I wouldn't hear any of it from Mario. Was I jealous of him? Absolutely. Was I insecure and way out of line? You bet. Was I full of pride, and full of myself? Yep. There was no excuse for my behavior. I wasn't myself. My frustration was really getting the better of me.

Things were bad then, but they were about to get a whole lot worse.

Entry #3

From Bad to Worse.

Later, I fell asleep pretty quickly. I'd had a tough day at the field, dealing with my jealousy towards Mario, and my own bees' growing frustration towards me. One thing that I've realized is that nothing gets anyone to sleep faster than exhaustion and frustration. You feel that and you pretty quickly go out like a light.

That night, I had the most wonderful dream ever. I dreamed of something completely different from my current situation at the server. Yeah, I was a total loser in real life, but in my dream, I had the biggest and most productive hive of all. I could see it glowing yellow in all its glory. It was a honey-making machine! The bees were all producing truckloads of honey and, most importantly, they were all happy. None of them were angry or frustrated with me. I had a wonderful working relationship with Nate and all the common bees. Better than that, I even had some legendary and epic bees to my name as well. The best part? I had an event bee! I had a real honest-to-goodness event bee! Not even Mario had that.

You can imagine just how happy I was. I'd have been happy to stay asleep forever!

"How's everything at the hive, Nate?"

Nate was smiling proudly at me. His smile stretched from ear-to-ear, and he looked way more than just pleased. He was really proud and beaming.

"Everything's running smoothly, boss! The hive has reached, well, epic proportions, no pun intended. Our epic and legendary bees are just pumping out that honey like crazy."

"Wonderful, wonderful! I'm so glad to hear that."

"Well, I also admit that we've been doing great work because of the hive's new event bee. We've got a gummy bee!"

"Wow! That's amazing!"

It was really wonderful news. An event bee hatching from one of the eggs was already rare in itself, but a gummy bee? Wow, this was awesome! It was wonderful to have this rare event bee on my side. Take that, Mario!

"Everything's looking up, boss!"

"Great! You know something, Nate? I'm really sorry if I was a bit too hard on you and the boys before."

In my dream, I really felt the need to apologize to my bees. After all, they were working very hard at this, and I had been pretty cruel to them. They clearly didn't deserve that kind of treatment, and yeah, I was sorry for it.

Nate shook his head and smiled at me. He was really very understanding.

"That's quite all right, boss. I mean, that's all in the past now. Besides, everyone gets a little angry now and then and loses it, right? Me and the boys don't hold a grudge against you if that's what you think."

"Thanks, Nate. I really appreciate the hard work and understanding. A guy like me doesn't deserve it."

Nate shook his head.

"Nonsense, boss. We're here for you and we'll always make you proud."

"Wow. You guys are the best ever."

"Boss, wake up!"

"What? What's going on?"

I was shaken out of my dream rather rudely. I opened my eyes, still a little sleepy and confused. Awake now, I realized that it had all been a dream. I wish it could have lasted a little longer.

"Sorry to wake you up boss, but we've got some real problems here!"

I looked up and saw the yellow figure of Kaz. Kaz was one of the many common bees in my hive. He was a very excitable sort who was made easily nervous and scared all the time. Because of his personality, I really didn't take his warnings too seriously. After all, Kaz had spilled and wasted a lot of honey more than once simply because he was so excitable.

"What's the big deal waking me up like that, Kaz? I was having the best dream ever, and you just interrupted it!"

"I know, boss! You were smiling, and I could tell you were having a good night's rest, but this simply couldn't wait! It's Nate! He's gone!"

"He's what?"

I sat up on the bed, now wide awake. I was so shocked at the news that I had to get up and start moving. I heard it but I couldn't believe it. Nate was gone! When it rains, it really pours. My hive simply couldn't afford for anything like this to be happening. I mean, nothing was working out for me already, and now this had happened. My only fairly good bee was gone. I simply couldn't let this happen.

"What are you talking about, Kaz?"

"I'm serious, boss! We looked everywhere in the hive. Nate's gone! It's like he just vanished or something!"

I stood up from my bed and ran around the hive looking for Nate. Kaz was right behind me. I looked around desperately and asked every single bee if they'd seen him. Unfortunately, Kaz wasn't just having some kind of nervous breakdown here. After searching the hive and asking everyone thoroughly, I had to admit the terrible truth: Nate was gone.

"Where could he have gone, boss?"

"I don't know, Kaz. I just don't know."

I felt terrible. At the back of my mind, I couldn't help but think that I kind of deserved this. It was pretty obvious why Nate would do something like this. Kaz didn't want to tell me to my face, but we all knew the real score here. Nate ran away because I was yelling at him and treating him like garbage. The poor bee had simply gotten fed up with me. Honestly, I couldn't even blame him.

"This is just awful. Nate was our best bee."

"He was a rare bumblebee, boss. He wasn't just a common bee like the rest of us" Kaz said.

"Don't say that, Kaz. You and your fellow bees are important to this hive."

Kaz gave me a kind of pained look. It was almost as if he had slipped and sprained his ankle or something. That is, if he could even sprain his ankle in the first place. Did bees even have ankles at all? I don't know. Well, the point is, he looked really hurt.

"Really? Can you really say that we're important to you, boss? You were just, well, a Noob in this game, and we all still joined with you. We all did our best to make the hive great, even if you were still new to all of this. Everyone tried their best, especially Nate.

But you always got on our case, including his. Can you really believe what you just said?"

Ouch. Well, Kaz was really straight to the point here. I guess I deserved it too. I wasn't exactly the best beekeeper recently. Everything that Kaz said was true. I had treated all of my bees so badly, it wasn't really surprising that Nate would just up and run off like that. Considering how I treated them all, I was lucky that they didn't all run away like Nate.

"I.. I don't know what to say, Kaz. I, I.. guess you're right. I have been treating you all really badly. I'm sorry."

There really wasn't anything else to say. It was pretty tense and awkward at the same time. I felt terrible for how I had been treating them, and now Nate was gone too. This was really getting bad.

Entry #4:

And then...

When Kaz told me that Nate had run off like that, I knew what I had to do. I wasn't really looking forward to doing it, but Nate was gone and I had no choice but to swallow the bitter pill.

"Mario, Nate's gone. I need your help."

Yeah, you guessed it. I went to Mario for help. I didn't want to, but what choice did I have? Mario was the best player in the entire server, so if anyone could help me, it had to be him. If he didn't want to help me, well,

I guess I really couldn't blame anyone but myself.

"Yeah, I thought you would come to me soon. Actually, Nate approached me, before he ran away."

"He what?"

"Yeah. He approached me all right. He was asking how to find that legendary tool that I was mentioning to you. That tool that could really increase hive productivity. He said that he wanted to get it to please you, Noob."

I couldn't believe what I was hearing. Nate had approached Mario before he ran off and Mario hadn't even told me! Now I was really furious!

"He approached you? Why didn't you tell me?"

Mario shrugged his shoulders.

"I thought he wouldn't go through with it. I already told him how far away the tool was and how dangerous the quest to get it could be."

"Where is this legendary tool, and what is it anyway?"

"The tool itself is located in the Pine Tree Forest."

"The Pine Tree Forest? That field is far from here, and is guarded by..."

Kaz couldn't even complete his sentence. His voice was trembling now.

"It's defended by Mantises and Werewolves. Yes, I know" Mario said.

I had heard about the infamous Pine Tree Forest. Unlike most fields in the server, it was full of, well, pine trees. It was really dark in that field and it was hard to navigate around it. And the worst part? Well, Kaz was right. The forest was home to werewolves and mantises. It was way too dangerous for Nate to be going there. I had to get him back before anything happened to him.

"And the tool?"

"It's the Super Jelly generator. It's supposed to be an ancient machine that generates Super Jelly."

Super Jelly. It was supposed to be some kind of legendary item that was ten times stronger than Royal Jelly. No one had discovered it yet, but a lot of players whispered that it could actually be made. If Super Jelly could be made, that would really be a game changer. That was because bees loved Royal Jelly. It was also the key to generating a lot of rare, epic or legendary bees. If Super Jelly existed and was even stronger than Royal Jelly, who knows what it could do? Well, it was all a legend, and now Nate had run away because of it. That, and my own harsh and mean ways.

"This is all my fault. If I hadn't been so mean to my bees in the first place, Nate would never have run away. I have to get him back. I'm going to the Pine Forest" I said.

"You're not going alone. I'm going with you."

It was Kaz. This was a really big step for someone like him. Kaz was a nervous wreck all the time. He had a real reputation in the hive as a bee who would easily lose it. Honestly, he was the least likely bee to go on a dangerous mission like this. I guess he was really that much of a friend to Nate. And Kaz wasn't the only one who wanted to accompany me to the Pine Forest.

"I'm coming along too, Noob."

"You too, Mario? Why would you accompany us? This has nothing to do with you. If anything, it's my fault that Nate got into this mess."

"Not really, Noob. If I hadn't told him in detail about the Super Jelly generator, Nate wouldn't have run away. I should have already known that he would be only too eager to please you. I guess you were right, Noob. I guess in a way, I just decided to mind my own business because I was the top player around here. I kinda got insensitive too."

I didn't want to drag Mario into my own mess but he was really insistent.

"Mario, you don't have to go with us..."

Mario shook his head.

"I do, and you're not stopping me, Noob. However, I do need to get a change of duds. I'm not going in there with my red and blue suit and my big belly. They might mistake me for some kind of a silly plumber or something."

Kaz and I looked at each other and chuckled. After all, it was a simple enough thing for Mario to get a change of clothes, but his belly, well, let's just say that no one loses weight in less than a day.

"Just give me a moment to prepare..."

"Take all the time you want, Mario. This is going to be a pretty dangerous quest."

"It will probably be dangerous, but it will be worth it, Noob! Who knows? We may even find that Super Jelly generator in the forest. If we do, I'm giving it to you!"

Mario ducked behind his hive as he spoke. He disappeared from our view, and Kaz and I could only assume that he was changing clothes.

"You don't have to do that, Mario. The

important thing is that we get Nate back safely."

"No, I insist. After all, I'm a little responsible for his disappearing like this too. You were right, Noob. I think I should have tried to help you get better in the game. After all, what are neighbors for?"

"Mario, I don't know... thanks, but let's just make sure Nate is safe first, alright?"

After a few moments, Mario reappeared. He looked completely different. His red and blue trousers were gone, and his moustache was completely shaved off! He now wore a yellow suit, complete with some wings on his back. They were just decorations of course; Mario couldn't really fly, and he wasn't a bee, but he definitely looked a lot different now. The best part? His belly was gone!

"Whoa! Mario, you're..."

Mario smiled at me and Kaz. He was savoring our looks of amazement.

"I lost weight? Yeah! What do you think of the new look?"

"You look completely different! You really look like a Roblox man now!" Kaz said.

"How did you do it? I mean, how did you...?"

"Lose the belly? It's okay, Noob. You can say it. I don't mind."

"Yeah, that. How did you do it, Mario?"

"Simple! I just took a good swallow of my hive's honey. My bees produce really great honey with amazing effects! Swallowing my hive's honey is a lot better than eating some magic flower!"

"What? What do you mean?"

"Never mind. Let's just go find Nate!"

It was settled right then and there. The three

of us would look for Nate. Maybe we would find the Super Jelly generator, maybe not. That wasn't really important to me. What was important was the safety of my rare bee. I realized that I had been really mean to him and all my other bees. I was aware now that getting better at the game wasn't worth becoming such a mean dude, and I didn't want Nate to pay for my attitude problem. I just hoped that we could find him in time.

Entry #5

The Attack of the Ants.

Getting to the Pine Forest wouldn't be easy. The three of us knew this and we prepared ourselves as best as we could. To get there, we would have to get past the Cactus field, and then the Pumpkin field. These two fields were guarded by werewolves, so we were already sure to encounter the things before we even got to the Pine Forest. Yeah, that was a very comforting thought.

We hurried out of our field and left right away. The three of us knew that we couldn't wait. Time wasn't on our side here. The sooner we found Nate, the better. There were just too many dangers everywhere, and we had to make sure that Nate was safe. I didn't even want to think about the possibility that something had already happened to him. I had to believe that we would find him. If we were too late, I would never forgive myself.

It would be a long way to the Pine Forest. We traveled along the long and wide Dandelion field first. It was the first of a few fields we would have to go through before reaching the Pine Forest. This was a field that was full of dandelions, just as the name said. The field was littered with the flowers and it was really easy to wander around and enjoy yourself if you were a bee.

"This is definitely the first field that Nate would have passed through. I'm sure of it, simply because I'm a bee too, and I would have done the same thing" Kaz said.

"I know what you mean. The smell alone is so wonderful; I'm sure it would be irresistible for him" I said.

It was so relaxing walking through that field full of dandelions. The smell was so easy on the nose, and having all those pretty flowers all around you was really very comforting.

"I could just stay here and collect pollen all day if we weren't looking for Nate."

"I know what you mean, Kaz. This dandelion field is really easy on the senses. Nate definitely passed through here. It's simply in your bees' nature."

Our appreciation of the dandelion field was cut short when we felt the ground shaking suddenly beneath our feet.

"Whoa! What's going on? It feels like an earthquake!" Mario said.

The ground was shaking so badly that we

could both barely stay standing.

"I'm really glad I don't have any legs or feet to walk on the ground with!" Kaz said.

"Yeah? That won't really matter if you get squashed with that thing!"

I was the one who noticed the giant ant first. It was so massive that every step it took made the ground shake and tremble. For something so huge, it was quite strange, because we never saw it coming. It was almost as if that big lug came out of nowhere.

A giant ant was the worst thing that we could have stumbled upon. It was the rarest of ants in the whole server. Despite this, it was clearly the most dangerous. One stomp of its several huge feet and we would be squished like bugs.

"Where did that thing come from?" Kaz said.

"Does it matter? Let's just get out before it

steps on us!"

We made a break for it, but it was too late. The giant ant saw us and, well, it wanted to stomp on us right then and there. Still, that wasn't the end of our troubles. Along with a giant ant came the inevitable swarm of ants.

"The ants are swarming behind him! This is bad! This is really bad!" Kaz said.

"What are we going to do now, Mario? I doubt even you could jump over that giant ant and trample him! Even if you did, there are so many other ants there that you couldn't possibly stop all of them at once!"

"I think I have just the thing!"

Mario whipped out a giant jar from his person. I really don't know how he managed to carry it with him during the journey. Who knew what he had brought along with him and what he could do with it? This was Mario we were talking about here after all...

Mario tossed the giant jar away from us. The jar shattered, revealing what appeared to be a lot of Royal Jelly. It wasn't just Royal Jelly, however.

"How did you manage to place all that Royal Jelly inside a single jar like that?" I asked.

"It's not just Royal Jelly; it's Royal Jelly mixed with my own hive's honey. The resulting mix is a lot denser than you can imagine, and you can stuff a lot of it into the jar. It's also super sweet, and ants of any size love anything that's sweet."

Mario was right. The moment he shattered the jar, all the ants ignored us and swarmed around it. They simply couldn't get enough of the stuff. The giant ant trampled upon several of the smaller ants just to get at the sweet puddle that Mario had tossed their way. A lot of the small ants were squished,

39

but there were more than enough to take their place. I couldn't believe it, but the ants were all fighting for that small puddle of sweet goodness.

"Amazing! They're all fighting for it! You're really something else, Mario!"

"You can praise me later. Let's just keep running now that their attention is off of us!"

It was a brilliant move by Mario who had managed to throw the ants off our trail.

"Boy, you really can do anything, can't you, Mario?"

Yeah, that was me there, gushing like a baby girl with a crush. I just couldn't help myself. I know I was really hard on Mario's case at first, but things were different now. They had to be; I mean this was the second time that Mario saved my skin from a monstrous mob. I was so glad that he was on our side.

"Thanks for the compliment, Noob, but I'm not immortal, perfect, or anything like that at all. I'm really just here to find Nate, like you and Kaz."

"And we'll do that. We've got to find him!" I said.

"I sure hope so."

The three of us looked back after we had put a considerable distance between ourselves and the ants. We heard in the distance the sounds of munching and trampling. The ground underneath us shook really badly, but as we gained ground, the tremors got weaker and weaker. Soon enough, we were way past the ants and they had completely forgotten about us. They were too busy eating up that mixture that Mario had prepared. Well, that was one obstacle we had overcome. I just hoped that we would be strong enough to overcome anything else that came our way and still find Nate.

Entry #6

The Werewolf.

After we got past the ants and the dandelion field, we approached a field that was vastly different from the previous one. While the dandelion field was full of attractive flowers and wonderful smells, this one was noticeably different. There weren't any flowers in this field at all, and it looked pretty barren. The field looked hot, dry and parched. There was nothing that grew here except for several cactuses that were spread all over the field.

"Whoa! What is this place?" I asked.

"This is the cactus field. This is the field that's closest to the Pine Tree Forest. We're getting close," Mario said.

Well, that was definitely a relief. After the experience with the giant ant and the other ants, I really just wanted to get back home and tend to my bees. I could see that Kaz was also getting nervous and going back to his old, jittery self.

"I sure can't wait to find Nate and get back home," Kaz said.

"Same here. I just can't wait to get back home. I don't want to face any more hostile mobs than we have to."

"Well, in that case, I really hate to disappoint you both, but there's probably a hostile mob guarding this field. I heard reports that a werewolf guards the cactus field," Mario said.

"Yeah, it's really reassuring," I said.

Despite our fears, we all advanced towards the cactus field.

The cactus field was, well, full of cacti everywhere we looked. You would have thought that we would have gotten pricked or nipped by all those spikes. Well, we didn't, not with Mario around. He surprisingly knew his way around this sharp field.

"You seem to know your way around here," I said.

"Yeah. I tried harvesting pollen here with my bees once, but I gave up after several tries."

"You giving up? Somehow, I can't seem to imagine that," Kaz said.

"I agree with Kaz. You seem to know how to take down just about every mob, Mario. Why did you give up harvesting this field?"

"Well, as you can both see, the field isn't really ideal. It's full of cacti, and it's also incredibly hot here. I probably could have made a go of it, but it wouldn't have been worth the effort, even if I did manage to get a good amount of pollen with my bees."

I wiped my forehead. The sweat was dripping from my head in buckets. Mario was right. It was pretty hot here, all right.

"I can see what you mean about the heat," I said. "I guess it would have been pretty tough harvesting this field."

"Believe me, Noob. If you want your hive to grow, it's best that you make the most of the common fields all over the server, just like the one we have. Just stick to it, and your hive will grow and produce a lot of honey in time."

I guess there was a lot of merit to what Mario said. I just couldn't really completely go for it because, I admit it, I was still pretty envious of all his achievements in the game. Well, I tried to set my jealousy aside. After all, it was that jealousy that got Nate in trouble in the first place. It was best to just let it go completely.

"I guess you're right, Mario. After all, you do have a lot of experience tending to a hive."

"You'll get there, Noob. Trust me."

The three of us approached the end of the field and came across a single cave. It looked really dark inside.

"This is where the field ends. What's inside that cave?" I asked.

"Well, uhm, this is the end of the field. The cave leads out of the field and towards the pumpkin field."

"And one step closer to the Pine Forest and Nate!" I said.

"Yeah. But we'll all have to get through that cave."

Mario turned towards it, and I could detect some fear in his voice. That was new. Mario seemed like the fearless type, and I wasn't used to seeing him show even a little fear and hesitation.

"Something wrong, Mario?" I asked.

"Nothing. It's just that, that cave is where the werewolf in this place lives. Or so they say."

"Yep. That doesn't sound very reassuring at all," I said.

"Come on, guys. We all have to keep going. We can't stop now. Nate's depending on us."

Mario was right. We had to enter that cave and keep going, even if we were more than a little afraid of what we might find inside.

"Well, bees first!" I said.

I motioned for Kaz to enter, and he just fluttered around us. Yeah, he wasn't going in there first all right.

"I'll go in first. You guys watch my back."

It was Mario. He went right in that dark cave, and Kaz and I followed. He carried this really big torch to light the way. It gave us a lot of light, and we could see right in front of us now. The light from the torch made entering the cave a little more bearable. We were all afraid, but being able to see in front of us made a big difference.

We kept walking for some time through that cave. It seemed to be quite long and wound around like some large snake.

"This cave seems to stretch to forever!" Kaz said.

"Don't worry. It will end. It's got to. And

when it does, we'll reach the pumpkin field."

"Wait a minute, Mario. You did say that you tried to start a hive here at the cactus field, right?"

Mario nodded.

"Yeah. What about it?"

"I don't get it. I thought you had already been there. Didn't you go inside this cave?"

Mario shook his head.

"I said that I went to the cactus field. I didn't say that I explored the cave here. This cave is completely new territory, even for me."

"So, you've never been here? How did you even know about the werewolf?" Kaz asked.

Mario shrugged his shoulders.

"Stories from other Bee Simulator players. They all talked about this really scary werewolf that guarded the cactus field. They mentioned that he lived in this cave. I never really stayed long enough to find out if there was any truth to the stories."

"I see. So you've never seen or encountered the werewolf yourself?"

"Exactly, and I would really hope to keep it that way."

Kaz smiled and fluttered about with some excitement.

"Well, we've been walking through this cave for some time, and we haven't caught a glimpse of any werewolf so far. Maybe it's all one big story. I mean, you know how it is? Maybe the werewolf is just a story to keep everyone away from the cactus field. Maybe we won't encounter him at all!" he said.

"I really hope so, but we've already encountered a ladybug and a giant ant and his fellow smaller ants. I wouldn't bet on the werewolf being nothing but a myth."

"Come on, Mario! Don't say that. Let's think positive here," I said.

"Let's just be ready for anything."

Sound advice coming from a true beekeeper like Mario, for sure. However, there was no way we would be ready for what would come at us right then and there.

It was the werewolf. He came at us from out of nowhere. Even with the torch in front of us, we still never saw him coming. His speed was amazing.

Suddenly, it was right in front of us. It was large and had a fearsome growl.

"Yikes! The werewolf!"

We all did the most logical thing. It was really the only thing anyone could have done. We ran out of there. More accurately, we ran away in the opposite direction of the werewolf.

We ran as fast as we could and we could hear the werewolf howling from behind us. We were all scared, even Mario. This was the first time I had really seen Mario scared. For the longest time, I had seen him as some kind of amazing player who could do anything. I guess it turned out that he was a lot more similar to me, or anyone else for that matter, than I had first thought.

"That's the scariest werewolf I've ever seen!" Kaz said.

"Is there really such a thing as a werewolf that isn't scary?" I said.

Kaz and Mario didn't answer. That was my point, exactly.

We kept running but, right at that moment, the werewolf suddenly appeared in front of us. I don't know how he did it, but it always seemed as if he were one step ahead of us and could pop up from out of nowhere. Did he have some kind of magical powers? I would later learn that there was a much simpler explanation for this than I thought.

The werewolf in front of us gave out a loud roar. This roar was even scarier than the last one and echoed throughout the whole cave. I covered my ears and shook in terror. This dangerous mob was right in front of us, and there seemed to be no way out.

"Don't eat us, please!" Kaz said.

And that was when it happened. I closed my eyes and raised my arms in front of my face, kind of expecting the worst. What I got wasn't the worst. It wasn't even anything any of us ever really expected at all.

"Eat you guys? I'm not going to eat you at all. I don't like eating things alive!"

The werewolf spoke to us in a very friendly and civilized voice. It was miles away from the bellowing cries that he gave out. He actually sounded like some kind of gentleman. None of us could believe what we were hearing.

"What the...?"

"Did you just say that you wouldn't eat us?"

It was Mario who gathered the courage to ask the werewolf about his motives. The werewolf continued to answer in a friendly tone that was miles away from his howls of terror.

"Why would I want to eat you guys at all?"

"Uhm, you did howl and growl earlier. What did you expect us to think?"

It was me asking this question. I couldn't understand any of it, so I just had to ask the werewolf up front what this was about.

"That stuff earlier? You guys were scared of that stuff? Come on! That's just how werewolves say 'hi.' I was surprised that you guys ran off when I was just introducing myself so I chased after you all. I finally managed to corner you."

None of us could believe what the werewolf was saying. This was something else.

"For real?" I asked.

"Why would I want to eat you guys?"

"For starters, you're a werewolf and that's what everybody thinks about werewolves. Everyone knows that werewolves eat anything alive," Kaz said.

"Oh, is that so? So, you're going to believe everything that everyone says about me and my kind? That is really incredibly mean of you to do so. So, if everyone said that bees were evil creatures that only wanted to sting people to death, you would believe them?"

"No way! That's different! Nobody thinks that way of us! We're all known for being cute and cuddly hardworking creatures that make honey all day!"

I nudged Kaz in the back.

"Uhm, actually he's right. Some guys actually do think bees are mean."

"For real? No way, boss!"

"Noob's right, and I kind of get what the werewolf is saying. Maybe he isn't as dangerous as we thought," Mario said.

"That's better. You guys can't believe everything they say about us. By the way, I'm not just "the werewolf " here. I've got a name too you know. I'm Melvin."

Melvin stretched out his paw to us. For a moment, I thought that he would rake or claw us with it, but it became apparently clear that he just wanted to shake hands, or paws, with us.

"Uhm, nice to meet you, Melvin. I'm Noob, and this is Mario, and my bee, Kaz."

"Nice to meet all of you guys. I'm glad you were all passing down here. After all, I don't really get too many visitors in here."

"That's not really surprising, but yeah, I get it," Mario said.

"Well, what brings all of you here?" Melvin asked.

"We're looking for a bumblebee. He's my bumblebee actually. A pretty fat one with a nice smile, and pretty friendly too. His name's Nate. Maybe Nate passed through here?"

Melvin reacted with excitement at my inquiry.

"Yeah! Yeah, I spoke with Nate earlier."

"Really? What did he say?"

"He said that he was looking for the way to the Pine Forest. He said that he was looking for the legendary Super Jelly generator."

Now I was excited too. We were on the right track, and there was still a good chance that we could find Nate.

"That's wonderful! What did you tell him?" I asked.

"I told him to go past the pumpkin field. The pumpkin field is just outside this cave, but you could get lost in this cave because there are many side routes and tunnels here. I know the way out since I live here. I showed Nate the way out. I could do that for you guys, too."

"You would do that? For real?"

Now I was really excited. We all were. This werewolf, or Melvin, had actually spoken with Nate. This was a really big development. Perhaps he was the key to finding and saving Nate.

Entry #7

The Giant Mantis.

Melvin was kind enough to honor his word and show us the way out of the cave. Melvin was actually a very friendly sort, just as he had described himself. He was in no way the terrible or terrifying werewolf that the stories made him out to be. Because of this, I did feel kind of guilty for immediately judging him as some kind of scary, fearsome creature. I could see now that Melvin was actually a very kind and friendly guy. Remind me never to judge someone in the future until I really get to know them better.

"Boy, this cave sure is confusing! There are a lot of tunnels and it's so dark. It all looks the same to me," Kaz said.

"That's just what I said earlier. The cave has so many twists and turns inside that it's easy to get lost in it. I showed Nate the shortcut out of here, just as I'm showing you guys."

After some time, we finally came to the end of the cave.

"Well, here we are. This is the end of the cave, and this is where the pumpkin field starts."

We reached the end of the cave, and just outside was a field full of pumpkins. It was just as Melvin had described it. We were really getting close to Nate now.

"Just get past this pumpkin field and you'll get to the Pine forest. I better accompany you guys all the way."

Mario shook his head.

"No, you don't have to, Melvin. You've already done enough for us by showing us the way out of your cave. We don't want to take up any more of your time. You've probably got something better to do."

Melvin shrugged his shoulders.

"Yeah, like what? It's not like a werewolf like me has a busy schedule or anything. I really don't have anything better to do. Besides, I think you guys are still going to need my help."

"Why is that so?" I asked.

"Well, because we're approaching the pumpkin field, and it's guarded by a mantis."

"Oh no! I had almost forgotten about that mob! There's always got to be some kind of dangerous creature blocking our way, hasn't there?" Kaz said.

"Well, if you insist, Melvin. We really could

use all the help we could get," Mario said.

We all walked through the pumpkin field. There were pumpkins as far as the eye could see. I was amazed at all the fields that the server had to offer. For the longest time, I was just stuck in my field with my hive, and with Mario and his. I kind of thought that the world was just limited to us. Boy, was I ever wrong.

"All these pumpkins look so yummy! It would sure be great to get pollen here!" Kaz said.

"I wouldn't really recommend that, Kaz. After all, this is the pumpkin field, and there is a big, bad mantis that lives around these parts," Melvin said.

"Well, I'm sure you'll be able to protect us if ever it shows itself."

Kaz didn't have long to wait for that. Before Melvin could say anything in response, we came across the giant mantis. It was lying behind a considerably large pile of pumpkins that were stacked on top of each other. Just as we passed the pumpkin stack, the mantis knocked all of them down, exposing himself to us. He was, well, a giant mantis. He was a little bigger than the giant ant, and that said a lot about his size!

"Whoa! That's the biggest mantis I've ever seen!" Mario said.

"You guys get moving! I'll distract it! Don't stop for anything! Believe me, it's not as friendly as I am," Melvin said.

"No way! We're not leaving you behind!" I said.

"Don't be silly, Noob! That giant mantis really will eat you guys up if you give it the chance, and there's no reasoning with it!"

I shook my head. I was firm about this. After

all, I had already lost Nate because of my bad attitude. I wasn't going to get Melvin in trouble for it too.

"That giant mantis isn't going to be easy to stop! How are we going to stop it?" Kaz asked.

"Exactly my point! That's why you guys should have run while you had the chance!"

Mario shook his head. Now I was seeing the old Mario again. There was no fear in his eyes, even with the giant mantis standing right in front of us.

"Noob's right! We're not leaving anyone behind here, not after what happened to Nate! Besides, I think stopping the mantis is a lot simpler than it seems!"

"Is that so? How?"

Melvin was getting a little frantic now. The giant mantis swiped at him with one of its giant legs. He leapt away just in time to avoid being swatted away like a fly.

"The answer is all over us, literally! Grab some pumpkins and throw them at the mantis!"

"I get what you're trying to do, Mario! It's brilliant!" I said.

Melvin did say that the mantis was crazy about pumpkins, and pumpkins were just about everywhere in the field around us. I grabbed some pumpkins and tossed them towards the mantis. They immediately drew the attention of the creature who started to munch on them.

"It's working! Keep tossing the pumpkins!" Mario said.

"Amazing! You guys sure are smarter than you look!" Melvin said.

Before long, even Melvin got into the act and started tossing pumpkins towards the mantis. It was so distracted that it couldn't even think of fighting anymore and, tossing a final load of pumpkins towards him, we strolled out of the field.

"Amazing that it completely forgot about us once it focused on the pumpkins!" Kaz said.

"A giant animal like that mantis is easily distracted," Mario said.

"Exactly! Now you guys can go straight to the Pine Forest. As I'm here with you guys too, I might as well join with you and go on all the way."

I could really see now that Melvin was anything but a scary werewolf. If anything, he was a friendly dude. I was really happy to have him come along with now as we neared the end of our journey.

Entry #8

A Great Surprise.

Well, we made it to the Pine Forest. This was the last stop in our journey to find Nate.

"Well, we're here. Now, we just have to find Nate and we can get back home," I said.

"If we find the Super Jelly generator, it could be a really big thing for all of us," Mario said.

I shook my head.

"If we find it, it's yours, Mario. I really don't care about that legendary item anymore. All I care about is the safety of Nate."

"You've really come a long way since we started out in this journey, boss. Nate will be glad to see that you're not who you used to be," Kaz said.

It was a grim reminder from Kaz, even if he didn't mean it. We wouldn't even be in this situation if I had been nicer to Kaz, Nate, and all my other bees in the first place. I just hoped that we were not too late.

The Pine Forest was full of trees; it seemed impossible to find a bumblebee like Nate in a large forest like this.

"How are we going to find Nate now? This forest is so big!" Mario said.

"Leave that to me! As a bee, I know Nate's particular scent and I can zero in on him through that, even in a place like this," Kaz said.

"Well then, it's up to you now, Kaz. Can you

catch Nate's scent?"

Kaz flew up into the air and sniffed around for what seemed like an eternity. Finally, he answered me.

"I've got it! Follow me!"

Kaz flew as fast as he could towards the scent. We all followed close behind him.

"I heard that there are werewolves here too! What are we going to do if any of them come out of the trees?" I asked.

"Leave them to me. You're with a very sociable wolf here. They won't harm you as long as I'm with you guys," Melvin said.

"Are we getting closer, Kaz?" Mario asked.

Kaz kept sniffing the air around him. His wings fluttered furiously and sounded more like a plane's propellers than wings. I had never seen him fly this fast and with this much purpose.

"We are! Come on, Nate's down here!"

We dashed through a lot of bushes and plants. I almost stumbled along the way trying to keep up with Kaz, but we all kept going and it paid off.

"He's here!"

Kaz led us straight to Nate. I was so relieved that he was all right.

Nate turned and saw us, and I could see the fear in his eyes. I really regretted seeing it there. It was my fault that he was so scared. I had treated him so badly and I was sorry about that. I knew that I had to change.

"Nate! You're all right!" I said.

"Boss! Kaz! Mario! And Melvin, too! What are you guys doing here?"

"Never mind that! I'm just glad you're all

right!"

I ran up to Nate and hugged him. Kaz came with me, and it was a group hug now.

"Boss, are you all right?"

"I'm fine, Nate! Listen, I know I've been really mean to you and the other bees, but I'm not going to do it anymore. I've realized the error of my ways. I'm not going to treat you like trash anymore. From now on, things are going to change around the hive!"

"For real, boss?"

I could see the look of shock and confusion on Nate's face. I guess he couldn't really believe that I was serious. After all the times I was so mean to him, I guess I couldn't really blame him for that.

"Yes. Don't worry, Nate. I mean it."

"Thanks, boss. I'm really sorry I ran off, but

I was looking for the Super Jelly generator. I didn't find it. I'm not even sure it's a real item."

I shook my head and smiled at Nate.

"I told you, Nate. That doesn't matter now. You guys just keep up the good work at the hive. I'm happy that you're all my bees."

"Thanks, boss. Really. Thanks."

"Look, guys! Maybe we can still go home with something after all!"

Kaz pointed to a small egg on the ground. No one had noticed it at first because it blended in with all the other rocks around it. We moved the rocks and saw it clearly. I couldn't believe what Kaz had found!

"Look, boss! It's a Tabby egg!"

"That's a rare event egg, Noob! That hatches into a Tabby bee! An event bee! That means..."

I smiled at Mario.

"That I'll finally have an event bee. Yeah."

"I'm so happy for you, Noob!"

So, I managed to get an event bee after all. That was all great and wonderful but, for me, it was just a bonus. The important thing was that Nate was safe, we all went home happy, and we even made a new friend in Melvin. It was a really great adventure that ended well for everyone!

The End.

If you enjoyed this book, please leave a review on Amazon! It would really help me with the series.

Best,

Robloxia Kid

Made in the USA
San Bernardino, CA
27 April 2020